HISTORY DETECTIVES

ANCIENT EGYPT

HISTORY DETECTIVES

ANCIENT EGYPT

WRITTEN BY PHILIP ARDAGH
ILLUSTRATED BY COLIN KING

PETER BEDRICK BOOKS
NTC/Contemporary Publishing Group
NEW YORK

First published in the United States of America in 2000 by
Peter Bedrick Books
a division of NTC/Contemporary Publishing Group
4255 West Touhy Avenue
Lincolnwood (Chicago), Illinois, 60712-1975, USA

ISBN 0-87226-629-X

1 3 5 7 9 8 6 4 2

Printed in Singapore

**The publishers would like to thank the following for their
permission to use photographic material reproduced in this book.**

1/2 title Werner Forman Archive(WF); title page cl, tr WF, bl AKG London(AKG),
c Robert Harding Picture Library(RHPL); contents page AKG; pp8br, tr, 9c,b AKG; p9t E.T.
Archive(ET); p10t SIGMA; pp10b, 11t AKG; pp11b,13b British Museum, London (BM); p13t WF;
p15t AKG; pp15b,17b ET; p17t BM; pp19t, 21t AKG; pp19b, 21b, 23t & b, 25t, 27t WF; pp25b, 27b
AKG; p29t Peter Clayton, b BM; p31t AKG; pp31b, 33t & b WF; pp35t & b , 37b BM; pp37t, 38b
AKG; p38t ET; p39t UNESCO; pp39b, 40tl/1, bl AKG; p40tl/2 Highclere Castle, tl/3 Hulton Getty
Collection, br Griffith Institute, Oxford; p41tl RHPL, tr Giraudon; pp42bl, 43tr BM; pp42br, 43br
AKG; p43tl Peter Clayton, bl RHPL

CONTENTS

ANCIENT EGYPT

Life in Egypt grew up around the river Nile. The Nile not only gave people fresh water and an easy route to travel along but also, after flooding each year, it left behind rich, fertile soil which was ideal for planting crops.

At one time, Egypt was two different countries: Upper Egypt and Lower Egypt. In about 3000 BC, which is around 5,000 years ago, they joined together under one ruler named King Menes. From that time on until 30 BC—almost 3,000 years later—Egypt was one of the richest and most powerful countries in the world.

3,000 YEARS OF HISTORY

Historians have divided Ancient Egypt's history into different periods. During all of this time Egypt was ruled by kings, queens and pharaohs—although some of them were "outsiders" from other lands. Then, in 30 BC, it became part of the Roman Empire.

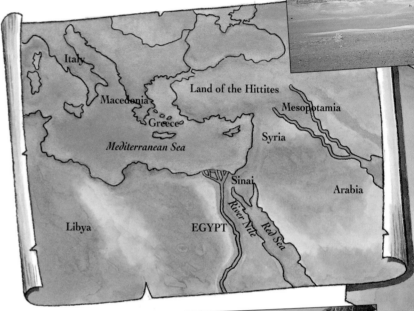

THE VALLEY OF THE KINGS

DIFFERENT PERIODS OF ANCIENT EGYPTIAN HISTORY

The Archaic Period	c. 3100 BC – 2649 BC
The Old Kingdom	c.2649 BC – 2150 BC
First Intermediate Period	c.2150 BC – 2040 BC
The Middle Kingdom	c.2040 BC – 1640 BC
Second Intermediate Period	c.1640 BC – 1552 BC
The New Kingdom	1552 BC – 1069 BC
Third Intermediate Period	1069 BC – 664 BC
The Late Period	664 BC – 332 BC
The Macedonian kings	332 BC – 305 BC
The Ptolemies	305 BC – 30 BC

c. is short for "circa" which means "about."

THE PYRAMIDS AT GIZA

THE SPHINX AT GIZA

MEDITERRANEAN SEA

Rosetta
Alexandria

Giza

Memphis
(Old Capital)

LOWER
EGYPT

SINAI

Most Egyptians
lived on the banks
of the Nile. This was
called the "Black Land,"
because of the rich soil
left behind after the
river flooded.

River Nile

RED SEA

Valley of the Kings

Karnak
Thebes
(New Capital)

THE TEMPLE AT KARNAK

Nearly all of Egypt was the
"Red Land." That is what
Ancient Egyptians called the
desert. Very few people could
live there, except around oases.

UPPER EGYPT

Aswan

Abu Simbel

THE GREAT TEMPLE AT ABU SIMBEL

CHANGING TIMES

In the days of the Old Kingdom, Egyptians believed that only kings could move on to the Next World after death because they were gods. It was during this time that the first pyramids were built as their tombs, including those at Giza.

In the Middle Kingdom period, Egypt became even more organized and new laws were made as trade with other countries grew. Beliefs also changed. Now Egyptians thought that anyone could go to the Next World after death so long as their dead bodies were prepared in the proper way and Osiris, one of the gods, judged them to be good enough.

It was during the New Kingdom period that kings were called pharaohs. Instead of being buried in pyramids, they were buried in tombs cut into the rock face in a place called the Valley of the Kings. The now-famous boy-king Tutankhamun lived at that time.

DISCOVERY

Ramesses II's body survives today, thanks to the skill of the Ancient Egyptians who mummified him, and the French scientists who destroyed a fungus that was eating away his remains in the late 1970s. It is on display in Cairo Museum.

Ramesses II ordered many carvings made in his image. This is a part of one of four giant figures cut into the stonework on the front of the Great Temple at Abu Simbel.

FAMOUS NAMES

Today, the boy-king Tutankhamun—who ruled over 3,000 years ago—is probably the most famous of Ancient Egyptians. But that's because of the incredible treasures that were found in his tomb in the early 20th century—not because of anything he did for Ancient Egypt. You can find out more about him on pages 40 and 41.

RAMESSES, WARRIOR KING

Ramesses II, however, was very famous in his own lifetime. He came to the throne in the 13th century BC, 48 years after Tutankhamun's death. Ramesses II ruled over Egypt for 67 years and lived to the remarkable age of 90. In fact, he outlived his twelve oldest sons, each of whom might have expected to become pharaoh after him! He had many wives and, probably, over 200 children.

Ramesses not only ordered the building of many temples, fortresses and palaces but he was also a great warrior. His most famous battle was for the city of Kadesh. Tricked and outnumbered, Ramesses managed to hold off the Hittite enemy while he waited for reinforcements. When they arrived, his army was victorious. Ramesses made sure that the official version of events carved onto temple walls had him winning the battle all on his own!

ALEXANDER, MIGHTY CONQUEROR

Another ruler of Ancient Egypt who was a legend in his own lifetime was the mighty general Alexander the Great. From a country called Macedonia, he invaded Egypt in 332 BC, at a time when Egypt was being ruled by the Persians. Alexander freed Egypt from Persian rule. This made him popular and he was crowned as the new pharaoh. In return, he was careful to respect the Ancient

Egyptian way of life. The city of Alexandria was founded by Alexander the Great and was named after him.

CLEOPATRA, ANCIENT EGYPT'S LAST QUEEN

After Alexander died one of his generals, called Ptolemy, became king. Ptolemy's descendants then ruled Egypt for the next 275 years, right up until Egypt fell to the Romans in 30 BC.

The last Ptolemy to rule Egypt was Queen Cleopatra VII, who ruled jointly with her brother. When she came to power in 50 BC, Egypt had lost many of its lands to invaders and was in decline. Julius Caesar, ruler of Rome, fell in love with Cleopatra and she tried to use her influence with him to increase her own strength. Rome was the most powerful country in the world.

But Julius Caesar was murdered in 44 BC and his adopted son, Octavian, had other plans for Egypt. Cleopatra, meanwhile, had married Caesar's friend Mark Antony. When Octavian's army defeated Cleopatra's troops at the Battle of Actium, she and Mark Antony killed themselves.

With its queen dead, Egypt became a part of the Roman Empire. The rule of kings and pharaohs was at an end.

HOW WE KNOW

Historians and archeologists (people who dig up and study things from the past) have learned a great deal about Ancient Egypt from the Ancient Egyptians' paintings and writings, and from the items they left behind. Throughout this book, you will find "discovery boxes" showing just some of the buildings, statues, models and paintings that still survive today and help us to learn more about this incredible ancient civilization.

DISCOVERY

This mosaic is of Alexander the Great. It shows him in battle, on his horse, as a brave and heroic leader.

Cleopatra's head is stamped on this coin. It was Ptolemy I, who used to be Alexander's general, who introduced gold, silver and bronze coins to Egypt.

THE PHARAOHS

Pharaohs were the kings of Egypt. They were very rich and powerful. The pharaoh owned the whole country and everything in it, including all the people. According to myth, the very first pharaoh was Re, the sun god. All other pharaohs were supposed to be descended from him, which meant that they were gods too.

The pharaoh could have many different wives, but only one could be the queen. Most pharaohs were men but some were women, including Hatshepsut, who called herself "king."

The pharaoh and his queen went to watch important events, such as the completion of an obelisk.

The pharaoh wore different crowns. This one was the double crown of Upper and Lower Egypt which symbolized that he ruled the whole of Egypt.

A platform and canopy was often put up especially for a pharaoh's visit outside the royal palace. It would be taken down when he left.

The queen was often carried on a special chair on poles, called a litter, but the pharaoh usually traveled on his chariot.

The pharaoh's private guards went with him everywhere to protect him.

Scribes recorded important events on special paper called papyrus.

High priests attended important events.

12

Obelisks were tall, pointed columns which were built to honor the gods. They were carved with the name of the pharaoh who ruled at the time.

The pharaoh had many servants.

Fans were made from dyed ostrich feathers.

Everyone had to bow down in front of the pharaoh. They often kissed the ground.

architect

Obelisks were carved from single pieces of stone and took many years to make. They were carried along the Nile by boat and then dragged across land and put in place. Each one weighed many tons.

DISCOVERY

This picture of the pharaoh Tutankhamun and his queen, Akhesenamun, is made of gold, inlaid with colored glass. The rays of sunlight shining down on the royal couple show the power of the sun god, Re. The queen is wearing a crown of ostrich feathers. This picture is actually the back panel of a throne found in the pharaoh's tomb.

Called an ankh, this symbol could only be carried by pharaohs and their queens, or — in pictures and statues — by gods and goddesses. It was the Egyptian sign for Life. The Egyptians believed that he who carried the ankh held the power of life and death over other people.

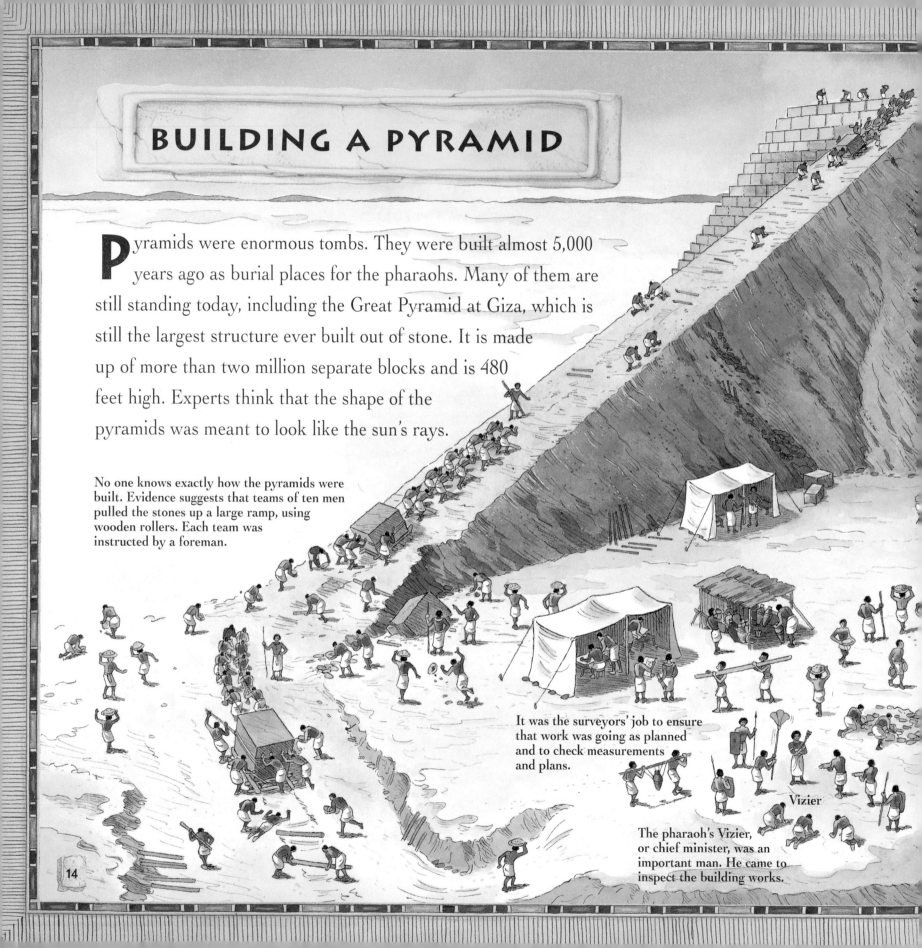

BUILDING A PYRAMID

Pyramids were enormous tombs. They were built almost 5,000 years ago as burial places for the pharaohs. Many of them are still standing today, including the Great Pyramid at Giza, which is still the largest structure ever built out of stone. It is made up of more than two million separate blocks and is 480 feet high. Experts think that the shape of the pyramids was meant to look like the sun's rays.

No one knows exactly how the pyramids were built. Evidence suggests that teams of ten men pulled the stones up a large ramp, using wooden rollers. Each team was instructed by a foreman.

It was the surveyors' job to ensure that work was going as planned and to check measurements and plans.

Vizier

The pharaoh's Vizier, or chief minister, was an important man. He came to inspect the building works.

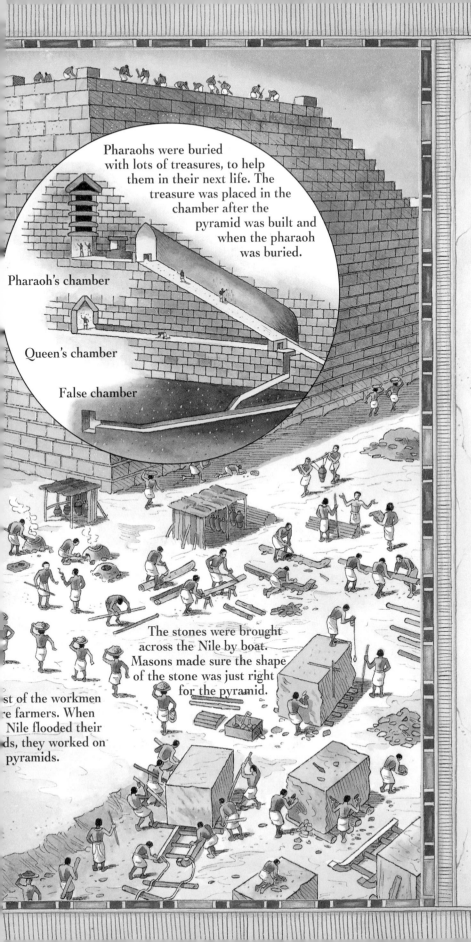

Pharaohs were buried with lots of treasures, to help them in their next life. The treasure was placed in the chamber after the pyramid was built and when the pharaoh was buried.

Pharaoh's chamber

Queen's chamber

False chamber

The stones were brought across the Nile by boat. Masons made sure the shape of the stone was just right for the pyramid.

st of the workmen e farmers. When Nile flooded their ds, they worked on pyramids.

DISCOVERY

The Great Pyramid at Giza was built about 2530 BC for a pharaoh called Cheops. The remains of the final layer of smooth limestone can be seen at the top. Today, all the pyramids in Egypt are empty. Every single piece of treasure was stolen within one thousand years of the pyramids being built.

This gold-covered mask of an important woman comes from the Valley of the Kings. It was here that later pharaohs and their families were buried, in tombs which were cut into the cliffs. The Egyptians thought that the treasures would not be stolen from these deep tombs.

MUMMIFICATION

Royalty, noblemen and people with enough money had their bodies mummified when they died. This was a special way that the Ancient Egyptians treated their dead so that their bodies would survive for life in the Next World.

Bodies were taken to an embalming (another word for mummification) shop called a wabet. Here, the innards were taken out and kept in special sealed pots called canopic jars. The bodies were then filled with sawdust, salt and herbs, covered in natron, sewn up and wrapped in bandages. This method of mummification was so good that many bodies have been preserved up to the present day.

The liver, lungs, stomach and intestines were taken out and put into four canopic jars. The heart was left in the body because it was needed for the journey to the Next World.

Good luck amulets were wrapped between the bandages.

A death mask was placed over the face of the mummy. The masks of rich people were covered with gold.

A priest, wearing the mask of Anubis, said prayers over the body. Anubis was the jackal god of the dead.

The wabet was where most of the work to turn a dead body into a mummy took place.

16

The body was then filled with sawdust, sweet-smelling herbs and a special kind of salt called natron.

The corpse was inside a layer of bandages, a death mask, an inner coffin and an outer coffin.

The face of the person was painted on the coffin so that it could be recognized in the Next World. It was then placed in a large stone coffin called a sarcophagus.

The body was packed in natron to dry it out for a few days before it was bandaged. It was this salt which stopped the bodies rotting.

Coffins found in pyramids came from an earlier time. They were much simpler wooden boxes.

DISCOVERY

Not only Ancient Egyptian people were mummified— Ancient Egyptian animals were too. Probably the most frequently mummified animals were cats. Cats were considered to be sacred animals and were loved and respected. Other animals to be embalmed included dogs, baboons and even crocodiles. Millions of mummified animals have been found over the years.

Amulets such as this one, shaped like a falcon to represent the god Horus, were often wrapped between the layers of bandages of a mummy. The Egyptians believed that they would bring the good luck of the gods to a corpse on its journey to the Next World.

THE AFTERLIFE

The Ancient Egyptians called the afterlife the Next World, or Kingdom of the West. It was believed that the dead person had to go through a number of tests to get there. Many people were buried with scrolls called The Book of the Dead. This was like a guide to help them on their way to the Next World which was ruled by the god Osiris. At the end of this journey, in the Judgement Hall of Osiris, the heart of the dead person was weighed against the Feather of Truth. If the feather and heart balanced, the dead person could then carry on to the Next World. If they did not, the heart was fed to a monster and the dead person could not enter the Next World.

All the possessions the dead pharaoh might need in the Next World — a place thought to be like Egypt only much more beautiful — were carried, together with his coffin, to the burial place in a huge procession.

The canopic jars were carried in large golden chests.

A chief priest burned incense. It was believed that the smoke carried the prayers to the gods.

Professional mourners cried and wailed at funerals. It was their job to mourn the death of the person. The more important the dead person, the more mourners he or she had.

The wadjet eye was painted on the side of boats to protect them on their journeys.

New Kingdom pharaohs were buried in the rockside tombs in the Valley of the Kings.

Furniture for the Next World.

Pharaohs were buried with their chariots.

Large barques were rowed by twenty oarsmen, and were steered by a man who controlled the huge rudder.

The coffin rested under a canopy.

Funeral barques such as this carried the bodies of pharaohs and queens along the Nile to their tombs.

DISCOVERY

Here, in the judgement hall of Osiris, a dead man's heart is being balanced against the Feather of Truth. If the dead man has lied about how good he was in life, his heart will be heavy and he will fail this final test. His heart will be fed to Ammut, the gobbler (sitting on the right), and, instead of life in the Next World, he will become an evil spirit.

The wadjet eye was supposed to be a symbol both of the sun god Re's eye, and the eye of the god Horus. Horus is said to have had an eye ripped out by Osiris's wicked brother Seth which magically grew back again. The Egyptians believed that the wadjet eye protected everything around it. This piece of jewelry, buried with a pharaoh, is in the shape of the wadjet eye.

GODS AND GODDESSES

Bes, the dwarf god, was very popular. He looked after the Egyptians' houses and their children. He was very funny.

The Ancient Egyptians believed in hundreds of different gods and goddesses. Each god or goddess ruled over a different part of life, from water to children to justice. Some gods were worshiped in small shrines, others were worshiped in huge temples.

During the New Kingdom, many impressive temples were built. Temples were busy places, often with workshops, schools and libraries. But in the inner sanctuary, only the priests and sometimes pharaohs performed holy ceremonies. Most ordinary people watched religious processions from outside the temple.

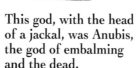

This god, with the head of a jackal, was Anubis, the god of embalming and the dead.

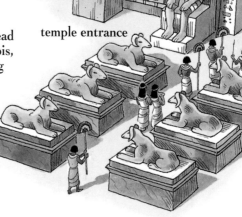

temple entrance

The lioness-headed goddess, Sekhemet, was goddess of motherhood and the deadly powers of the sun.

Sobek, the god of water, had the head of a crocodile. The Nile was full of crocodiles.

Outside many temples were "avenues of sphinxes" — sphinxes were statues of creatures with lions' bodies and human, or often rams,' heads.

Re, the sun god with a hawk's head, created the world. Once, when he cried, his tears turned into a swarm of bees.

Obelisks were carved with the names of pharaohs and writings about Re.

This was Amun-Re, king of the gods. "Amun" means "hidden." He had many powerful secrets.

This was Khnum, who had a ram's head. He made people out of clay on his potter's wheel.

Ma'at, with her beautiful wings, was the goddess of truth and justice.

This bronze statue of the cat goddess Bast is over 2,500 years old. Unlike many gods and goddesses who were shown with human bodies and the head of a particular animal, Bast was shown as a complete cat. She represented the healing and crop-ripening powers of the sun.

The ruler of the Next World was Osiris, shown here on a wall painting. He ruled the kingdom of the dead under the earth which was believed to be like Egypt but even more beautiful.

LIFE IN A VILLA

Rich and powerful Egyptians lived in grand country houses, such as this one, called villas. A villa was built from mud bricks, and the walls were then covered with plaster. Inside, they were often painted with bright colors. The house was kept cool because the small windows only let in a little sunlight. The outside of the villa was painted white to reflect the heat of the sun away from it.

Extravagant banquets were held in the main hall.

Visitors arrived through the gatehouse so the gatekeeper could see who went into the villa.

Often there was a fish pond in the center of the garden.

22

Chariots and horses were kept in the stables.

Villas needed wells for a supply of fresh water.

Shrines were used by families for private prayer.

Grain was stored for safekeeping.

Kitchens were well away from the house.

Bread was baked outside.

DISCOVERY

Only very rich Egyptians had furniture such as this chair. It has copper fittings and is inlaid with gold. The chair was buried in a queen's tomb at Giza over 4,000 years ago. Rich or poor, most Egyptians sat on stools.

This wall painting shows people at a party wearing scented cones of fat on their heads. Ancient Egyptians often wore these cones, especially at celebrations. When the cones began to melt in the heat, the perfumed fat trickled down their faces, keeping them cool and making them smell good!

23

THE MARKET

temple

obelisks

Ancient Egypt was the richest country in the world. Some of its gold was used to trade with countries including Nubia and Syria. People traveled from far and wide to offer gifts to the mighty pharaohs, and the palaces were filled with spices, wines and treasures. Ordinary people who lived in towns could shop at the market. Here they could buy everything from fruit to jewelry. People usually bartered for goods—swapping them for other items. Money wasn't invented until late in Ancient Egypt's history.

At refreshment stalls, thirsty shoppers could buy a kind of beer which was as thick as soup.

Many goods were brought in from the countryside by donkey.

Fresh wine was kept in long, thin jars. They were sealed shut until it was time to drink it.

Markets were often on the edge of the Nile. This made it easy for ships to deliver their fresh cargo straight to the stalls.

Spices and grain were kept in sacks.

The Medjay used temple storerooms as prisons for criminals waiting to go to trial.

People living in towns often used their roof as an extra room.

Most stallholders were women.

Awnings kept the sun off the goods and the seller.

In their workshops, craftsmen made many different objects from metal and wood, including furniture, statues and jewelry.

The Medjay were a kind of police force. They caught criminals and brought them to trial.

DISCOVERY

This painting, from a wall of a tomb in Thebes, shows craftsmen in a jewelry workshop. They are drilling holes in beads, polishing them and making wide "wesekh" collars which were popular in Ancient Egypt.

Wooden models still survive showing the Ancient Egyptian way of life. This model is of brewers making beer, ready to sell at the market.

25

ON THE NILE

The Ancient Egyptian civilization grew up along the banks of the river Nile. It was the once-a-year flooding of the river that brought rich soil to the land—soil which was ideal for the planting and growing of crops to feed the people. Without the Nile, all of Egypt would be an empty desert because there is very little rain.

Every year (on about 15th July) the waters of the Nile rose. Only the villages, built on higher ground, stayed above water level. A clever system of dikes and channels was made to take the water to where it was needed most.

At the end of the growing season, the farmers harvested their crops in the spring. Half of the crops went to the pharaoh as "tax." This was used to feed people such as scribes, priests and craftsmen who didn't grow their own food.

All crops were grown on the thin layer of soil left by the Nile on top of the sand. These included vegetables, wheat, barley and flax.

One farmer's land was divided from another's by boundary stones. These stayed in place even during the floods.

If a stone moved, one of the pharaoh's surveyors had to put it back in place. Farmers could not move the stones.

Barley was used for bread and beer.

Water could be drawn from an irrigation ditch using a device called a shaduf. It had a bucket on one end and a weight on the other.

Flax was grown for making into clothes.

Ferry boats carried people across the Nile, rather than up or down it. They were often overcrowded.

Unlike a rich family's country villa, a peasant farmer's home was very basic.

It had one main room, shared by all the family. Peasants had very few possessions.

oxen

goats

geese

donkey

Fishermen used nets to catch fish. Rich hunters used spears called harpoons.

The Ancient Egyptians enjoyed hunting. Birds were often hunted with throwing sticks.

DISCOVERY

Many different boats used the Nile, from small private boats to trading ships and funeral barques. This is a model of a sailing boat with the pilot at the front and the owner resting under a canopy.

The man in this wall painting is harvesting the wheat crop using a tool called a sickle. The handle of the sickle was made from wood but the cutting edge was made up of a row of tiny sharpened flint "teeth." Flint is a type of stone. His wife is collecting the grain in a basket.

27

THE ARMY

For over 1,500 years, the Egyptian army was made up of a small number of full-time soldiers and the pharaoh's small group of bodyguards. If needed, ordinary men were called up to fight too but Egypt was generally at peace. However, during the New Kingdom, the Egyptians had to fight off a big invasion. This led to the growth of a large army and the development of new weapons and chariots. The pharaohs also began thinking about conquering other lands. The new army was divided into divisions of 5,000 men, made up of companies of 200 foot soldiers and 25 two-man chariots.

Each company had its own battle standard.

Each army camp had a shrine to the god Amun.

There was a man in charge of army pay. He also kept a written record of what happened in the company.

Doctors traveled with the company to care for the wounded after battle.

Sentries stood guard.

Army camps, such as this, were set up when the Egyptian army was on the move. The walls were made out of the soldiers' shields.

A ditch was dug to make the camp harder to attack.

A charioteer carried messages.

Body armor was introduced during the New Kingdom. The officer on the left is wearing strong leather armor.

Officers slept in tents with folding beds. Ordinary soldiers had to sleep outside.

DISCOVERY

Tutankhamun is shown here riding into battle on his war chariot. His enemies are falling under the feet of his two horses. To make him look more of a hero, Tutankhamun is shown fighting alone. In real life, he would have had a soldier to steer the chariot while he fired arrows at the enemy.

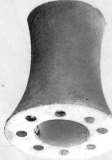

Archers sometimes wore a bone finger guard. This protected the finger when pulling back the string of a bow.

FOOD AND DRINK

Ancient Egyptians loved eating and drinking and there was plenty of food for the rich to choose from. They were served everything from fried fish to roast goose, along with fresh vegetables, lots of fruit and special breads. Favorite fruits were figs, dates and grapes.

Servants baked, boiled, fried, grilled, roasted and stewed delicious meal after meal. Most cooking was done outside, sometimes on the flat roofs — which could lead to houses catching fire. Everyone ate bread and most people drank beer but it was the rich who drank wine. The wines and beers were very sweet, and so was the bread. The dough was often mixed with honey, fruit or herbs.

Grapes were grown on trellises.

The grapes were trodden and the juice collected in jars for the best quality wine.

The juice of what was left of the grapes was then wrung out in a sack to make the less good wine.

Ducks and geese were roasted on spits.

Tripods were used for frying food.

Food could be stewed in huge pots on legs called braziers.

Fires were lit using something called a firedrill. Flames were made by rubbing the stick from side to side.

Beer was made in thick, flat-bottomed jars. Grains of barley and baked barley loaves were mixed with water and left to ferment.

30

Cool shady rooms were used to store wine. The tops of the jars were sealed to stop the wine going bad.

On the side of each jar someone wrote where the wine came from and when it was made.

Flavorings were often added to the dough when making bread.

Bread was cooked on the outside of ovens. When it was cooked, the dough stopped being sticky and the loaves fell off.

When it was time to serve it, the beer was so thick it had to be sieved.

DISCOVERY

This picture, from the tomb of a priest and scribe, tells us how the Ancient Egyptians made wine. It shows people treading the grapes. The juice then pours through a pipe in the side of the trough into a large basin.

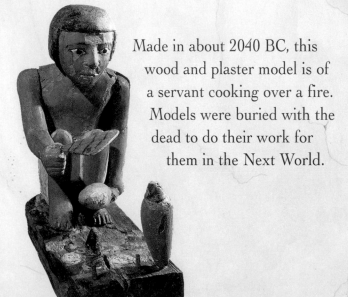

Made in about 2040 BC, this wood and plaster model is of a servant cooking over a fire. Models were buried with the dead to do their work for them in the Next World.

31

CLOTHES AND JEWELS

Men wore kilts. These were made of linen from a plant called flax. Some kilts were more fancy than others.

Ancient Egyptians loved looking their best. Everyone wore jewelry. It didn't matter if you were a man or a woman, rich or poor. The rich wore jewelry made from gold and semi-precious stones. The peasants wore jewelry made from glazed pottery. Most men and women also wore make-up around the eyes. They used a special dark green or grey paint called kohl. Kohl not only made people feel they looked more handsome or beautiful, it helped to keep flies away from their eyes too. As for clothes, it was so hot that most people wore very few — but fashions did change over three thousand years with clothes becoming longer and looser-fitting.

Both men and women wore beaded collars.

Most women wore simple white dresses, also made from flax.

Some men and women shaved their heads to keep cool and then wore wigs.

People often walked around in bare feet. Some wore sandals.

Over time, kilts got longer and clothes became looser with more flowing folds of material.

32

Women often colored their lips and cheeks with red soil, called ochre.

Some make-up boxes were shaped like birds.

A special chest contained a rich woman's mirror, comb, tweezers and small pots of kohl.

Hair was sometimes padded on special occasions to look fuller.

Boys' hair was often shaved except for a long braid at the side.

Women sometimes wore cloaks.

bracelet

rings

Some dresses were dyed different colors and even had glass beads sewn on to them to make them sparkle.

DISCOVERY

This beautiful glass fish is a bottle. It probably contained perfumed oil. Rich Ancient Egyptians would rub oil all over themselves to stop their skin cracking in the heat.

Jewelry as fine as this would only have been worn by a pharaoh or, perhaps, his queen. This belonged to Tutankhamun. Made from gold and semi-precious stones, the pattern is of scarab beetles and cobras. The largest scarab is shown holding up the sun.

LIFE AS A CHILD

The birth of a child was a very happy event in an Ancient Egyptian household, but many children died young. Boys and girls were loved and cared for. Most children didn't go to school. A few boys from richer families went to school in the mornings, usually at the local temple. Some girls were taught at home by their parents and learned to read and write. Children were encouraged to keep fit and had lots of different toys and games to play with. Some of the luckier ones had pets too. Boys who had been to school usually went on to a profession such as lawyer, scribe or doctor. Those children who stayed at home grew up to help around their town or village.

Girls had wooden and clay dolls.

Some wooden animals had moving parts.

Some children had pets, from dogs and cats to geese and even monkeys.

Balls were made of everything from clay to plant fibers.

Often children didn't wear any clothes. Sometimes they wore kilts or sleeveless tunics.

Spinning tops were popular toys.

Educated boys grew up to become scribes, priests, doctors, lawyers or officials.

Many children went into the family business, helped around the village or on the farm, or trained to be craftsmen.

Boys from richer families went to school.

pipe

hand-held cymbals

Girls could become priestesses, dancers, musicians or even scribes.

five-stringed harp

DISCOVERY

Pull the string on the head of this toy cat and its jaws snap shut. Some of its teeth are missing now but it could, when new, have given someone in Ancient Egypt a nasty bite!

This wooden horse is about 2,000 years old. The wooden wheels turn around and it was pulled along by a rope through the hole.

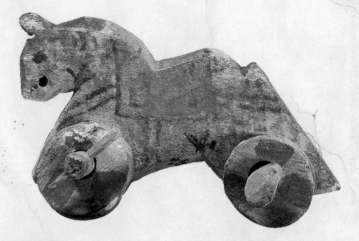

35

HIEROGLYPHS

The Ancient Egyptians were one of the first civilizations to have writing —but not many of them could actually write. Writing was left to the educated and particularly to scribes, who made a living doing it. Each scribe had to train for about twelve years to learn all the different letters and picture symbols called hieroglyphs—there were over 750 of them to remember! Some symbols stood for letters of the alphabet and some stood for numbers. Then there were special hieroglyphs which experts call determinatives. These are picture symbols which stand for a whole word—such as "enemy" or "village." Sentences were a mixture of letter and word hieroglyphs. They could be written from left to right, right to left or up and down.

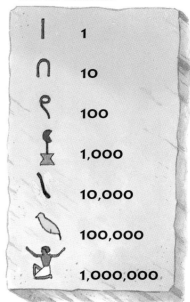

These symbols were used for numbers.

	1
	10
	100
	1,000
	10,000
	100,000
	1,000,000

This is how other numbers were made.

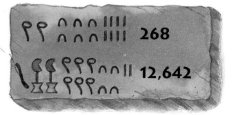

268

12,642

Scribes were very important people in Ancient Egypt and they kept records about almost everything. These hieroglyphs mean, *"Set your heart on being a scribe. You call to one and a thousand answer you."*

This message begins on the right. You can tell this because that's the direction all the characters in the hieroglyphs are facing.

TUTANKHAMUN

Pharaohs and queens had their names written in special picture groups called cartouches.

Here are some of the hieroglyphic letters.
The Ancient Egyptian alphabet didn't have any vowels.

B   D   F   G

H   K   M   N

P   Q   R   S

T   W   Y   Z

These are examples of determinatives – single
hieroglyphs with whole word meanings.

HOUSE   TOWN OR VILLAGE

GARDEN   SAVAGE

FRIEND OR REJOICE   RUN   ENEMY

GOD OR KING   GODDESS OR QUEEN

DISCOVERY

This statue is made from granite. It shows a scribe in the traditional cross-legged pose with a piece of papyrus on his lap. He is holding open the scroll with his left hand and would have been writing with the other. The statue is slightly damaged and his brush has been lost.

The Rosetta Stone is one of the most important finds in the history of Egyptian archaeology. Discovered in 1799, it is carved with the same text written in three different kinds of writing, including Ancient Egyptian hieroglyphs and

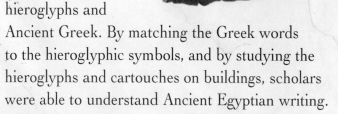

Ancient Greek. By matching the Greek words to the hieroglyphic symbols, and by studying the hieroglyphs and cartouches on buildings, scholars were able to understand Ancient Egyptian writing.

DISCOVERY

This is how the Sphinx at Giza looks today. Its nose survived for thousands of years, only to be shot off by a cannonball fired by Napoleon's army at the end of the 18th century.

Tutankhamun's treasures were only saved from 19th century robbers because the entrance to his tomb was buried underground, here in the Valley of the Kings.

DISCOVERING THE PAST

Archeologists are people who study the past, often by digging things up or looking at things which have been left behind. But, in days gone by, many so-called archeologists were nothing more than treasure-seekers who wanted riches and fame for themselves and their countries. Many artifacts—even whole buildings—were plundered from other countries and shipped "home."

Modern archeologists, however, are true History Detectives, piecing together the clues left by people in the past to try to build a picture of how these peoples used to live. These clues range from the smallest pieces of pottery to jewels, wall-paintings, statues and buildings.

TOOLS OF THE TRADE

Like modern police forces, archeologists now have many pieces of scientific equipment to help them in their detective work. By using a special instrument to measure how much carbon there is in an object, for example, it is possible to work out how old the object is. This very useful test is called carbon dating.

THE RIDDLE OF THE SPHINX

One of the monuments which has most puzzled archeologists is the Sphinx, a giant statue next to the Great Pyramid. Over 4,500 years old, the Sphinx has a lion's body and a human face. For centuries it was thought that there were secret passages inside the Sphinx. But today most archeologists are sure it is carved from solid rock.

ABU SIMBEL

As well as discovering and learning from ancient monuments and artifacts, archeologists have also done much to look after them. A dramatic example of this happened when, in 1956, the Egyptian government decided to build a new dam at Aswan, and to flood a large area of Egypt to collect water. Before this happened, archeologists from all over the world actually moved more than twenty Ancient Egyptian monuments to stop them being destroyed.

SEE-THROUGH BUBBLE

The greatest challenge was to try and save the temples at Abu Simbel. This was particularly difficult because they weren't built of separate stones but carved into the side of the mountains.

One suggestion was to cover the two temples with a giant see-through bubble. This was so they would be safe when the area was flooded, but they could only be seen by divers! This plan was rejected. It was too expensive and meant that most people would never get to see these very important Ancient Egyptian monuments.

CARVING UP A MOUNTAIN

Eventually, every carving was carefully cut out of the mountains at Abu Simbel in sections, and then put back together on the front of two human-made mountains. These were built to look like the temples' original surroundings — but safe from the flood waters when the new dam was built. This was done with complete success. Today, the temples look as if they've stood on this new site for thousands of years!

DISCOVERY

This huge face belongs to of one of the colossi (enormous statues) from the Great Temple at Abu Simbel. Carefully cut into sections and lifted by cranes, the temples were later put back together in their new home — safe from the waters created by the dam at Aswan.

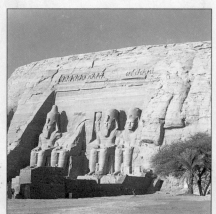

The Great Temple from Abu Simbel at its new safe site. Built to the glory of Ramesses II, each colossus is over 66 feet tall with a face over 13 feet wide.

THE TUTANKHAMUN DISCOVERY

Tutankhamun
Crowned pharaoh and married aged 9
Died when 16 or 17
Ruled Egypt over 3,000 years ago
1323 BC buried in the Valley of the Kings

Lord Carnarvon
George Edward Stanhope Molyneux Herbert
5th Earl of Carnarvon
Born 1866 Died 1923
Funded excavation that discovered Tutankhamun's tomb

Howard Carter
Born 1874 Died 1939
English archeologist
Led the team that found the tomb of Tutankhamun
with its fabulous golden treasures

THE BACKGROUND

Lord Carnarvon spent his winters in Egypt for his health. It was here that he became interested in Ancient Egypt. It was also here, in the city of Cairo, that he met Howard Carter, the great archeologist.

In 1912 Carter persuaded Lord Carnarvon to excavate the Valley of the Kings. This was the burial ground of the pharaohs during the New Kingdom. Most of these tombs had been robbed of their treasures long ago.

The Valley of the Kings

THE FIND

Ten years later, on November 4th, when local men working for Carter were digging in the valley, they discovered sixteen stone steps leading down to the closed entrance to the tomb of Tutankhamun. Carter sent Lord Carnarvon a telegram:

AT LAST HAVE MADE WONDERFUL DISCOVERY IN VALLEY; A MAGNIFICENT TOMB WITH SEALS INTACT; RE-COVERED SAME FOR YOUR ARRIVAL; CONGRATULATIONS.

When Lord Carnarvon arrived, this first door was opened. A dark rubble-filled corridor was cleared and a second sealed doorway, marked with Tutankhamun's name, was reached. On November 26, 1922, Carter took some stones out of this doorway, held up a candle to the hole and looked into the tomb. Carter wrote:

It was some time before one could see, the hot air escaping caused the candle to flicker, but as soon as one's eyes became accustomed to the glimmer of the light the interior of the chamber gradually loomed before one, with its strange and wonderful medley of extraordinary and beautiful objects heaped upon one another ... When Lord Carnarvon said to me "Can you see anything?" I replied to him "Yes, it is wonderful."

Tutankhamun's
solid gold mask

THE CURSE

Some people claimed that there was a curse on all who entered the tomb. There were certainly some amazing coincidences…

26 people were at the opening of the tomb. Six of them died within ten years. One of these was Lord Carnarvon, after a sudden illness. It is said that, at the exact moment he died, all the lights went out in Cairo and, back in England, his dog gave one last howl and dropped dead.

Carter's pet bird was eaten by a cobra the day the tomb was opened. There was a cobra on the pharaoh's death mask.

An expert traveling to X-ray the bones inside Tutankhamun's mummy died on the way there.

THE TREASURES

The tomb was full of amazing treasures — treasures which made it the most important archeological discovery in Egypt. Tutankhamun's mummy was wearing a solid gold death mask and lay in a solid gold coffin. The surrounding rooms were crammed full of everything from model boats and beds to precious jewels, chariots and a throne of beaten gold.

However the boy-king Tutankhamun was not one of the greatest pharaohs. His reign was very short and his advisers held much of the power. When Tutankhamun was buried no one could have guessed that he would become the most famous pharaoh of all.

AN EGYPTIAN
TREASURE TROVE

AMAZING FIND
IN EGYPT

ALADDIN'S CAVE

Most people working in the tomb were fine, however, including Howard Carter himself. The curse is probably just a good story.

This scarab beetle is one of the many precious jewels found in the tomb.

41

TIMELINE

- INVASION AND RULE BY THE HYKSOS
- NEW WEAPONS AND HORSE-DRAWN CHARIOTS INTRODUCED BY HYKSOS

C.3100 BC   C.2649 BC   C.2150 BC   C.2040 BC   1640 BC

THE ARCHAIC PERIOD
451 YEARS

- KING MENES UNITES UPPER AND LOWER EGYPT
- CAPITAL IS BUILT AT MEMPHIS
- HIEROGLYPHS INVENTED
- IRRIGATION BEGUN

THE OLD KINGDOM
499 YEARS

- THE FIRST PYRAMID IS BUILT—THE STEP PYRAMID AT SAQQARA
- CHEOPS BUILDS THE GREAT PYRAMID AT GIZA

FIRST INTERMEDIATE PERIOD 110 YEARS

THE MIDDLE KINGDOM
400 YEARS

- MENTUHOTEP REUNITES ANCIENT EGYPT
- CAPITAL IS MOVED TO THEBES
- A TIME OF STRONG AND POWERFUL RULERS
- THE FIRST KNOWN SCHOOLS ARE RECORDED

SECOND INTERMEDIATE PERIOD 88 YEARS

- TOMBS ROBBED
- GOVERNMENT COLLAPSES

The Rosetta Stone—the key to cracking hieroglyphs

The pyramids at Giza

Ramesses II's mummy

Coin showing the
head of Cleopatra

1552 BC   1069 BC   664 BC   332 BC   305 BC   30 BC

THE NEW KINGDOM
483 YEARS

- DEFEAT OF THE HYKSOS
- CAPITAL IS MOVED TO THEBES
- THE AGE OF MANY GREAT PHARAOHS
- HATSHEPSUT, THE WOMAN PHARAOH RULES
- RAMESSES II RULES FOR 67 YEARS
- TUTANKHAMUN BECOMES THE BOY KING

THIRD INTERMEDIATE PERIOD
405 YEARS

- WIDESPREAD CORRUPTION
- AT ONE TIME, ANCIENT EGYPT RULED BY FIVE KINGS AT ONCE
- NUBIAN KINGS RULED DURING SOME OF THIS TIME

THE LATE PERIOD
312 YEARS

- PERSIANS RULE ANCIENT EGYPT
- EGYPTIANS OVERTHROW PERSIANS AND SET UP SMALL DYNASTIES
- PERSIANS RETAKE ANCIENT EGYPT

MACEDONIAN KINGS 27 YEARS

THE PTOLEMIES
275 YEARS

- ALEXANDER'S GENERAL, PTOLEMY, BECOMES KING
- 31 BC ANTHONY AND CLEOPATRA ARE DEFEATED BY ROMAN FORCES AT THE BATTLE OF ACTIUM
- ANCIENT EGYPT BECOMES A PROVINCE OF THE ROMAN EMPIRE

- 332 BC ALEXANDER THE GREAT OF MACEDONIA FREES ANCIENT EGYPT FROM PERSIAN RULE
- ALEXANDER CROWNED PHARAOH
- CITY OF ALEXANDRIA FOUNDED

Tutankhamun's
death mask

Alexander the Great

43

THE PHARAOH'S STOLEN TREASURE

A MYSTERY ADVENTURE STORY

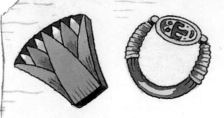  

YOUR MISSION

NEWS HAS REACHED THE PHARAOH THAT A PYRAMID HAS BEEN ROBBED. IT IS THE PYRAMID OF ONE OF THE GREATEST PHARAOHS, WHO HAD RULED EGYPT HUNDREDS OF YEARS BEFORE. THREE NIGHTS AGO, IN THE DARKNESS, SOMEONE BROKE INTO THE TOMB AND STOLE THE FABULOUS TREASURE. IT SEEMS THAT THE THIEF KNEW EXACTLY WHERE TO LOOK. HE—OR SHE—ENTERED ONLY ONE CHAMBER, WHERE THE MOST VALUABLE TREASURES WERE HIDDEN.

THE PHARAOH HAS TRAVELED FROM HIS PALACE, ALL THE WAY TO THE PYRAMIDS AT GIZA. IT IS THERE THAT HE IS WAITING FOR YOU. YOU HAVE BEEN CHOSEN TO FIND OUT WHO STOLE THE PHARAOH'S MISSING TREASURE.

HOW TO BE A HISTORY DETECTIVE

To help you solve the mystery, you will need to answer questions along the way. These can be answered using information in the first half of the book. Simply turn to the page number shown in the magnifying glass.

For example, **12** would mean that an answer lay somewhere on page 12.

These answers also earn you points, so that you can keep score. You'll find how many points an answer scores when you check yours against the answers on pages 58 and 59.

But you must do more than simply answer the questions to find out who stole the pharaoh's treasure. You must look out for clues in the words and pictures throughout this book too.

By the end of the story, you should be able to say who the thief is. You can find out if you are right by checking page 60. The right answer will score you an extra 20 points.

Add up all your points and find out how good a history detective you are (also on page 60).

Good luck!

YOUR MISSION BEGINS

You are led into a royal tent, pitched near the pyramids, and bow before the pharaoh and his queen. "I have summoned you to ask you to find out who stole the treasure from the pyramid of my forefather," he says. "You must not fail me."

A man steps forward. "Great pharaoh, let me find the thieves," he says. "I will bring them to justice, whoever they are."

The queen puts up her hand for silence. "Thank you, Hori, but, as leader of the pharaoh's guards, you're well-known throughout Egypt. For this task, we need a stranger." She nods towards you. You see a look of anger flare in Hori's eyes, but he bows gracefully.

"Now leave us," the pharaoh orders. Soon the tent is empty except for you, the pharaoh and his queen.

MOSI **NODJMET** **KAMOSE**

"Be careful who you trust," the pharoah says, showing you a papyrus, with pictures of three people on it. "These are the three suspects," he explains.

"Mosi, who used to be one of my generals . . . Nodjmet, the famous singer, dancer and musician . . . and Kamose, a scribe with some very powerful friends."

"Remember their faces, and take this," says the queen. She hands you a second papyrus. "It shows some of the pieces of missing treasure. We have arranged for a boy called Maya to help you. He's very clever and knows his way around. You'll find him at the wabet in the old capital city."
The pharaoh claps his hands, and a servant leads you from the tent.

What is a wabet? **16**   Where is the old capital? **9**

The first thing you see on entering the wabet is a group of people in the next room, standing around a table.

"You can't go in there!" calls out a voice.

You turn around and see a boy crouching down in the shadows behind some strangely-shaped jars. "Why not?" you demand.

"Because my uncle and the others are wrapping up a body, to make a mummy. The chief embalmer himself will be here soon. It's a very important occasion . . . and we're not invited."

You lower your voice. "I'm looking for Maya," you explain.

"And you've found him," grins the boy. "That's me."

When you explain who you are, he's very excited. "You actually met the pharaoh?" he asks. You nod. "I have to check you're not lying," he says. "So tell me what kind of crown he was wearing." You think back. Which crown was it? **12**

When you tell Maya about the crown, his face breaks into an even bigger smile. It seems to work like a password. "Right!" he says. "Then let's get going. I've been told to show you where Kamose the scribe lives. We'll take my uncle's donkey."

Soon you're riding bareback through the dusty streets of the town. You stop on the corner of a busy street. "This is Kamose's house," says Maya. "He tells everyone he's a man of peace but I've heard stories that he likes a good fight!"

You stand on Maya's shoulders and look through the first window. You can see a woman. She must be Kamose's wife. In her hands is a box shaped like a duck. It may not be part of the treasure, but what is it? (33) "Come on," whispers Maya. "You're getting heavy."

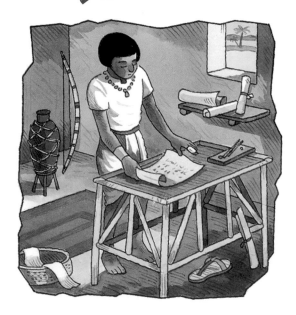

You look through the next window and see the suspect, standing by his desk. On his table is a piece of papyrus and some writing tools. But what's that strange thing that looks like a thimble on his finger? It strongly suggests that he hasn't been practicing his writing as a scribe, but something else. What has he been doing? (29)

Before you realize what's happening, Kamose has snatched up his bow and is sliding an arrow into place. The razor-sharp tip is pointing straight through the window . . . and straight at you!

"Spies!" Kamose growls, "This is my home! Go away!"

"Let's get out of here! Now!" Maya shouts. You run after Maya, back to the mule, and both leap on to its back. An arrow whistles past your ear, but soon you are far enough away to be safe.

Kamose is certainly not very friendly but that doesn't necessarily make him the thief. You decide to check out the other suspects. "I've heard that Mosi is planning a hippo hunt on the other side of the Nile today," says Maya. "Let's catch a ferry and go and see what's happening."

You ride to the banks of the River Nile, dismount and look out across the water. There are all kinds of boats. You turn to ask Maya which one is the ferry, but he's already leaving, on the mule. "We don't have much time," he shouts. "You find Mosi. I'm going to look for Nodjmet."

It's up to you to go to the hippo hunt alone. Mosi is a suspect and must be investigated. But first you must cross the river. Which of these boats is a ferry? **26**

The ferry is crowded with men, women, children and animals. You're surprised no one has fallen overboard . . . when someone does just that, with a loud SPLASH.

The nearest passengers quickly put out their hands and drag the person back on to the deck. She is a girl of about twelve and looks very frightened.

"I was pushed in on purpose!" she claims, but most of the other passengers laugh and turn away. "Somebody tried to drown me," she insists.

"Why would anyone want to do that?" asks a kind woman.

"Because of what I saw by the pyramids three nights ago," she sniffs. Your ears prick up. It was three nights ago that the pharaoh's treasure was stolen from the pyramid.

"What did you see?" you ask.

The girl, who says her name is Teti, tells you her story.

"I was tired, a long way from home, and I fell asleep by a rock.

When I woke up, I saw the shadowy shapes of two people.

They were dragging a chest out of a pyramid past a snoring guard."

50

You listen to Teti's story in amazement. She is an important witness to the crime. "Then what happened?" you ask.

"They spotted me! But I managed to escape," she says. "They were wearing long cloaks and carrying weapons, I think. I didn't get a chance to see their faces, but they don't know that."

"Can you remember anything else?" you ask.

"One of them dropped this," she says, pulling a small object from inside the folds of her wet clothes.

"Have you any idea what it could be?" (35)

THE HUNT GOES ON

Back on dry land, you wave farewell to Teti and arrange to meet her later. You have no trouble finding the hippo hunt. You can see a group of people in the water with spears. An angry hippo is showing off its massive jaws and huge teeth.

You could not have got here at a better time. Mosi, the ex-army general, has just arrived in his chariot and is now wading out to a raft. You notice nasty cuts on his legs.

"How did he get those?" you ask a man looking after his horses.

"From a fight he had in Uhrt, five days ago. Despite many wounds, he rode all the way back here on his chariot," he says proudly. "People gathered to cheer him on his way. Mosi's very brave and he's a great soldier."

Your attention is caught by yet another familiar face. It's Nodjmet, the second suspect on the pharaoh's list. You wonder what she's doing here!

She pushes her way through the crowd of onlookers. "Where's my servant?" she asks a small, bald man.

"Over by the shaduf," he replies in a loud whisper.

"Make sure I'm not followed," she orders. If you want to hear what she says to her servant, you must get there first. You look around. Which of these is her servant? (26)

You spot the shaduf and get there before Nodjmet, hanging back out of sight. "What news?" she demands.

"Not good, mistress!" her servant cries. "Hori must speak to you at once. He's waiting at the usual place." As she hurries back to her chariot you notice she's carrying something. But what is it? **27**

With the roar of the angry hippo still sounding in your ears, you climb into the back of Mosi's chariot. You can see the cloud of dust thrown up by Nodjmet's chariot as she races towards a town in the distance.

With a flick of the reins, you are in hot pursuit. Perhaps she will lead you to the missing treasure.

Your horse narrowly avoids the startled Mosi, who is talking to one of his men.

In the brief moment that your chariot flashes past him, you hear the words " . . . must speak to the Vizier . . . " above the noise of thundering horses' hoofs on the flat earth. The Vizier. Who is the Vizier? **14**

You need to keep your eyes on Nodjmet and her speeding chariot. What's happened to Maya? He is supposed to be following her. You enter the outskirts of town and see that she has left her battered chariot and panting horses by the roadside. You quickly leap from your own chariot and push your way through the crowds after her . . . doing your best not to be spotted. Then you lose sight of her. After all this, you've lost her! You're about to give up when you hear a passer-by say, "Wasn't that Nodjmet, the famous dancer, who's just gone down the avenue of sphinxes?"

What is the avenue of sphinxes? Where does it lead? **20**

You dash into the temple, then slow your pace so as not to attract attention. Inside it is dark and cool. You're just in time to catch sight of Nodjmet disappearing behind a brightly painted pillar.

A man appears at her side. It's Hori, leader of the pharaoh's guards. "I've locked that interfering Maya in the Medjay's prison. No one will think of

looking for him there!" he whispers. "Now we must go to the villa at Barub."

"Good work, Hori," says Nodjmet.

You must help Maya escape at once, but where is the prison?

After a few wrong turns, you see Maya through the bars of a window . . . but you are grabbed by Nodjmet and thrown into prison too. Maya is very pleased to see you.

"My uncle once told me that there's a secret passage out of here," he says excitedly.

"Where's the passage?" you ask.

"Look for the picture of Sobek," he says. "Press it, and it opens the entrance to the secret passage. Press a wrong symbol first, and we'll never get out — we'll be stuck here until Nodjmet decides what to do with us. The trouble is, I can't remember what — or who — Sobek is!"

Which sign should you press?

Free at last, you remember that Hori and Nodjmet were going to the villa at Barub, so you ride there on Maya's donkey. Maya stays on it. "You find out what Nodjmet and Hori are doing here," he says. "I'll try and find out about Mosi and Kamose . . . Good luck!" He rides off.

You enter the villa and make your way nervously to a large central hall. In the cool shadows of mighty pillars you watch groups of richly dressed men and women laughing and talking. It's a party!

Suddenly there is a loud CRASH.

"Halt!" barks a voice you recognize only too well. It belongs to Hori, who has tracked you down. "Take this uninvited guest away for questioning!" he commands.

A huge guard, with the strength of a hippo, grabs you roughly. At the same time, he slips you a note.

What does it mean? 37

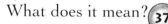

BEWARE OF ENEMIES

If this message is to be believed, at least this guard is friendly . . . but Hori is close behind. You are taken into the garden.

"Hide in the nearest grain store," whispers the guard. "I'll arrange for the man who tends the tears of Re to help you later." But where are the grain stores? **23**

You spy a store just as the friendly guard "trips" and falls to the ground, releasing you from his grip. You run to the grain store and into your hiding place. Holding your breath, you hear Hori searching for you in the garden. After what seems like ages, all goes quiet.

You come out from under a pile of grain and creep into the gardens.

All clear! But what should you do now? You look around for "the man who tends the tears of Re." The friendly guard had said he would help you.
Which is he? **21**

You spot the right person just as he spots you.

"Hori has guards at every exit," he says. "But I know a secret way out." You follow him. "Be careful," he urges. "Hori will do anything to lay his hands on that treasure."

Thanking the man for his help, you slip out of the garden through a hole in the wall. "Psst!" says a voice. It's Maya. He beckons to you from behind a clump of trees.

You follow him and tip-toe away quietly from the villa in the fading evening light.

"I have news," he says. "Back in Memphis, I heard one of the pharaoh's guards interviewing Kamose . . . Kamose said that he's never been anywhere near any of the pyramids ever — let alone inside one three nights ago."

"And where did he say he was when the pyramid was robbed?" you ask.

"He claims he was asleep on his roof," says Maya.

It's getting late. "In the morning, I think we should go to the scene of the crime!" you suggest. That is exactly what you do.

At daybreak, you set off with Maya on the back of the mule. "I haven't done so much riding since I went to Uhrt last year," says Maya. "From here, that's a three-day ride on the fastest horse but, with this old girl, it took six." He pats the animal fondly.

With no treasure left to rob inside, the pyramid is unguarded. You walk through a passage where the thief must have entered. Maya lights a torch and holds it up to guide you. You enter the chamber where the treasure used to be.

Suddenly, you hear a noise behind you. Hori steps out of the shadows, sword drawn. "Where's the missing treasure?" he demands. "Tell me, or I'll send you both to the Kingdom of the West!" he laughs.

Where is that? 18 What does he mean?

"Not so fast!" says another voice. It's Mosi. He knocks the sword from Hori's hand. "I may not be a friend of the pharaoh's any more, but only a coward attacks unarmed enemies," he snarls. "Be gone!" Hori doesn't need telling twice. He runs down the passage and out of the pyramid.

You look around the scene of the crime but you dare not move. "Is that your sandal?" Mosi asks, pointing.

"It's not one of ours," says Maya, shaking his head.

"Hmm," says Mosi, with a frown. "What are you doing here?" he demands.

"We were going to ask you the same question," says Maya.

Mosi laughs. "A brave one, you are. If you must know, I was thinking that if I could find out who stole the treasure, the pharaoh might give me my old job back. He should be told about Hori at once. I'll go and find the Vizier."

Of course, you've no way of knowing whether to trust Mosi or not. You don't hang around to find out and you leave the pyramid in a hurry.

Riding into town you see Kamose and his wife. They are helping a richly dressed man to load wine jars on to his chariot.

Recognizing you as you go past, Kamose says loudly, "I hope you enjoy the wine. It's fresh and well worth the price." But there seems to be something strange about the jars.

What is it? **24**

Once again, you find yourself in the presence of the pharaoh and his queen. You have brought Maya and Teti, the girl from the ferry, with you. This time Hori isn't there. He has been banished for disobeying the pharaoh, and is lucky to have escaped with his life. You're pleased to see that the guard who helped you escape in the villa garden has taken his place.

The pharaoh claps his hands and the three suspects are brought into the room.

The pharaoh turns to the suspects. "You are here to answer the charges laid before you by Maya and my special investigator." He points a royal finger at you. "One of you stole the treasure from the pyramid . . . and I have also heard stories of kidnap and imprisonment in the temple."

 "Oh mighty pharaoh, surely you're not going to take the word of Maya against mine, are you?" Nodjmet sniffs. "I'm a famous singer, musician and dancer! And who is that young girl? Why is she here?"

 "She's that girl who was hanging around the pyramids," says Kamose. "You're not going to listen to her, are you, great pharaoh?"

 Mosi points to you and Maya. "As nice as these two are, mighty pharaoh, you can't expect them to know who took the treasure, can you? They're not trained investigators or soldiers."

"Oh, but I do know which one of you is the thief," you say triumphantly. "I've been through the facts and I have the answer."

Who stole the treasure from the pyramid?

You can check your answer with the **SOLUTION** *on page 60*

ANSWERS AND SCORES

Next to each answer is a number. This is the number of points you should award yourself if you got the answer right without looking it up here in the back first. And there are extra points if you worked out who stole the treasure.

PAGES 48 & 49

- A wabet is an embalmer's shop, where dead bodies were mummified.   4 points
- The old capital city of Ancient Egypt was Memphis.   4 points
- The pharaoh was wearing a red and white crown.
  This is called the double crown of upper and lower Egypt.   6 points
- The duck-shaped box is a make-up box.   4 points
- The thimble-like object on Kamose's finger is a finger guard,
  worn when firing a bow and arrow. Kamose has been
  practising indoor archery!   6 points

PAGES 50 & 51

- The ferry is the boat full of people going across the river,
  rather than up or down it. So you get on this boat.   3 points
- The strange object that Teti saw the thief drop outside
  the pyramid is a single hand-held cymbal.   4 points
- The shaduf is a pole with a bucket on it, so the person in front
  of it is Nodjmet's servant. You go over to where he is standing.   6 points

PAGES 52 & 53

- Nodjmet is carrying a throwing stick. She probably brought
  it with her to go bird hunting.   3 points
- The Vizier is the pharaoh's chief minister.   3 points
- The avenue of sphinxes is the path lined with ram-headed
  sphinxes which leads to the temple.   4 points
- Hori says that he's put Maya in the Medjay's prison.
  The Medjay — a kind of police force — often used temple
  store rooms as prisons. That's where Maya will be.   6 points
- Sobek is the god with the head of a crocodile.   4 points

PAGES 54 & 55

- The message reads: Friend. Run. Garden. It means that the
  guard is friendly and will let you escape once in the garden.   5 points

- The grain stores are the cone-shaped stores.
  They are a safe place to hide.   4 points

- The "tears of Re" are the bees, so speak to the bee-keeper.   5 points

PAGES 56 & 57

- The "Kingdom of the West" is another name for the afterlife.
  Hori wants to kill you!   4 points

- The jars have no lids. If they had fresh wine in them, the jars
  would be sealed shut.   5 points

•TO FIND OUT IF YOU'RE RIGHT ABOUT WHO STOLE THE
PHARAOH'S TREASURE FROM THE PYRAMID, TURN TO
PAGE 60 AND TURN THE BOOK THE OTHER WAY UP.

Score 10 points if you guessed the right person.
Score 20 points if you found out who the thief was by working out all the clues correctly.

BUT WHERE IS THE MISSING TREASURE?
THE THIEF HID IT IN LOTS OF DIFFERENT PLACES. SOMETIMES IT
IS EVEN DISGUISED. IF YOU GO BACK THROUGH THIS ADVENTURE
STORY, YOU SHOULD BE ABLE TO FIND THE PIECES SHOWN IN THE
QUEEN'S PAPYRUS ON PAGE 48. HAPPY HUNTING!

SOLUTION

Mosi cannot have stolen the pharaoh's treasure. You know that the pyramid was robbed three nights ago (pages 46 and 50), and were told on page 51 that Mosi had a fight in Uhrt five days ago and rode back on his chariot. On page 56, Maya says that this journey is "a three day ride on the fastest horse." Mosi would have arrived back after the treasure went missing.

Teti, the girl on the ferry, saw one of the pyramid robbers drop a musical instrument. Nodjmet is a singer, dancer and musician. She kidnapped Maya, with the help of Hori, to stop him "interfering." Nodjmet and Hori were working together, but it's clear from the question he asks you in the pyramid that Hori doesn't know where the treasure is (page 56).

Maya said he heard Kamose claim that he'd "never been anywhere near any of the pyramids ever." (page 55) but he recognized Teti as "the girl who was hanging around the pyramids." (page 57). The discarded left sandal in the pyramid (page 56) matches the right sandal in his room (page 49). He must have left in a hurry! It was Kamose who stole the treasure with his wife. They were the cloaked figures Teti saw. They dropped the cymbal (page 51) to throw suspicion on Nodjmet, the musician. The other cymbal (they come in pairs) is on the table in Kamose's house (page 49). They sold the treasure, hidden in wine jars (page 57), to a rich merchant they first met in the villa at Barub. You can even see a piece of treasure sticking out of the top of a jar!

HOW DID YOU DO?

BETWEEN 90 AND 100 POINTS

Wow! When it comes to being a History Detective, you're the very best.

You're not only good at following the clues, but you worked them all out brilliantly. Well done.

BETWEEN 75 AND 89 POINTS

Excellent! You're true detective material. You worked well with the facts to solve the clues.

BETWEEN 60 AND 74 POINTS

Not bad. Not bad at all. You've got some way to go before you're a truly great detective, but you certainly know how to handle an investigation.

BETWEEN 50 AND 59 POINTS

OK, so you're not going to win any big-shot detective awards, but you're on your way to becoming a pretty good detective. Keep practicing!

LESS THAN 50 POINTS

Oh dear. A short spell at detective school wouldn't do any harm. Better luck next time.

GLOSSARY

Amulets — good luck charms, usually in the shape of gods, goddesses or sacred objects.

Ankhs — amulets in the shape of the symbol of life. These could only be held by royalty or shown in paintings and carvings as being held by gods and goddesses.

Boundary stones — stones marking the limits of farmers' fields. These could only be moved by official government surveyors.

Canopic jars — special jars containing the intestines, livers, lungs and stomachs of mummies.

Colossi — the plural of **colossus**, a huge statue.

False chambers — empty chambers inside pyramids designed to trick tomb robbers into thinking they contained treasure.

Hittites — rulers of a mighty empire in Northern Syria and Asia Minor.

Irrigation — a system of supplying water to crops by digging ditches and canals. Ancient Egyptians built a series of ditches and canals, leading off the river Nile, which could be opened and closed as needed.

Medjay — originally paid soldiers from Nubia, the Medjay became the Ancient Egyptian police force.

Mummification — turning dead bodies into mummies. The name comes from the Persian word "moumia," meaning bitumen (a kind of tar). Persians thought Egyptian mummies were covered with bitumen, but they were wrong.

Natron — a mixture of special salt used for drying mummies before they were bandaged.

Next World — another name for the Kingdom of the West or afterlife, ruled over by Osiris.

Obelisks — tall, thin monuments with pointed tops. Built to the glory of the sun god Re.

Papyrus — a kind of thick paper made from papyrus reeds.

Romans — originally from the city of Rome, founded in the 8th century BC in what is now Italy, the emperors created a huge empire and became the most powerful force in the "world."

Scribes — people specially trained to read and write. This was a very important job and they were very well paid.

Sphinxes — statues representing the sun god, usually with the heads of pharaohs or rams and the bodies of lions.

Vizier — the chief minister. The most powerful state official after the pharaoh.

Wabets — embalming shops, where dead bodies were mummified.

Wadjet eye — a symbol protecting all around it, it was made into amulets, jewelry and even painted on to sides of boats.

INDEX